Cool

REFASHIONED

SCARVES & TIES

FUN & EASY FASHION PROJECTS

ALEX KUSKOWSKI

Checkerboard
Library

An Imprint of Abdo Publishing
abdopublishing.com

abdopublishing.com

Published by Abdo Publishing, a division of ABDO, PO Box 398166, Minneapolis, Minnesota 55439. Copyright © 2016 by Abdo Consulting Group, Inc. International copyrights reserved in all countries. No part of this book may be reproduced in any form without written permission from the publisher. Checkerboard Library™ is a trademark and logo of Abdo Publishing.

Printed in the United States of America, North Mankato, Minnesota

062015
092015

THIS BOOK CONTAINS RECYCLED MATERIALS

Content Developer: Nancy Tuminelly
Design and Production: Jen Schoeller, Mighty Media, Inc.
Series Editor: Liz Salzmann
Photo Credits: Jen Schoeller, Shutterstock

The following manufacturers/names appearing in this book are trademarks: Tulip®

Library of Congress Cataloging-in-Publication Data

Kuskowski, Alex, author.
Cool refashioned scarves & ties : fun & easy fashion projects / Alex Kuskowski.
    pages cm. -- (Cool refashion)

Audience: Grades 4 to 6.
Includes index.
ISBN 978-1-62403-703-0

1. Scarves--Juvenile literature. 2. Dress accessories--Juvenile literature. 3. Fashion design--Juvenile literature. 4. Handicraft for girls--Juvenile literature. I. Title. II. Title: Cool refashioned scarves and ties.

GT2113.K87 2016
646.4'8--dc23
                    2014045321

To Adult Helpers

This is your chance to assist a new crafter! As children learn to craft, they develop new skills, gain confidence, and make cool things. These activities are designed to help children learn how to make their own craft projects. They may need more assistance for some activities than others. Be there to offer guidance when they need it. Encourage them to do as much as they can on their own. Be a cheerleader for their creativity.

Before getting started, remember to lay down ground rules for using tools and supplies and for cleaning up. There should always be adult supervision when using a sharp tool.

Table of Contents

RESTART YOUR WARDROBE

Reuse YOUR Wraps

Get started refashioning! Refashioning is all about reusing things you already have. You can turn them into new things that you'll love.

Do you have some old scarves and neckties? Use them to make headbands or bags. Or **transform** them into new-looking scarves and ties.

4

Permission & Safety

- Always get **permission** before making crafts at home.

- Ask whether you can use the tools and materials needed.

- Ask for help if you need it.

- Be careful with sharp and hot objects such as knives and irons.

Be Prepared

- Read the entire activity before you begin.

- Make sure you have everything you need to do the project.

- Follow directions carefully.

- Clean up after you are finished.

Basic terms and step-by-step instructions will make redoing your closet a breeze. These projects will help you turn neckwear into one-of-a-kind fashion pieces.

5

SUPER SCARF & NECKTIE fAShiON

Scarves and ties are made of fabric. Make something new out of the fabric from scarves and ties you already have.

You can cut, glue, sew, or dye fabric into something new. Don't let your neckwear be plain. Remake it to fit you!

WHAT TO MAKE WITH SCARVES

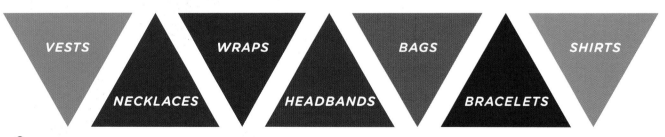

VESTS · NECKLACES · WRAPS · HEADBANDS · BAGS · BRACELETS · SHIRTS

Refashion Ideas for Neckwear

SUPER SCISSORS

- Cut old scarves or ties into strips. Braid the strips. Make a necklace or bracelet from the fabric.
- Cut your scarves or ties into patches. Sew them onto other clothing.

COLOR CHANGE

- Dye light-colored scarves any color of the rainbow.
- Draw on a dark-colored scarf with a bleach pen. Add a **design** all your own.

ADD SPARKLE

- Glue decorative gems onto a scarf with fabric glue.
- Sew a beaded trim onto a scarf.

SEW NEW

- Turn a scarf into a skirt or a bag.
- Turn a tie into a small bag or headband.

7

TOOLS & MATERIALS

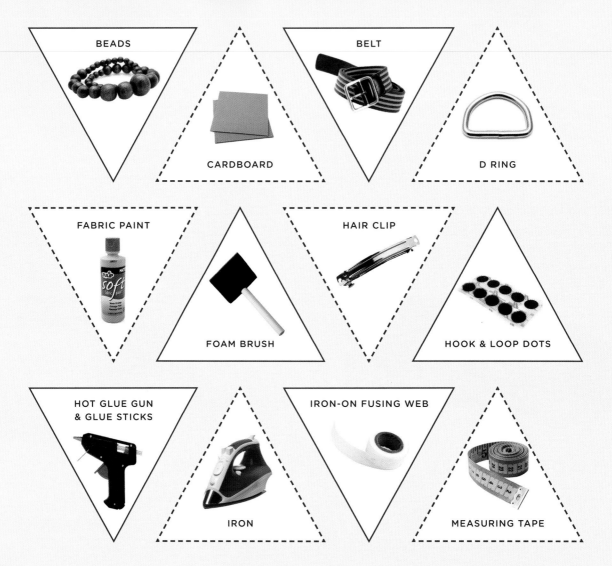

BEADS

CARDBOARD

BELT

D RING

FABRIC PAINT

FOAM BRUSH

HAIR CLIP

HOOK & LOOP DOTS

HOT GLUE GUN & GLUE STICKS

IRON

IRON-ON FUSING WEB

MEASURING TAPE

HERE ARE SOME OF THE THINGS YOU'LL NEED FOR THE PROJECTS IN THIS BOOK.

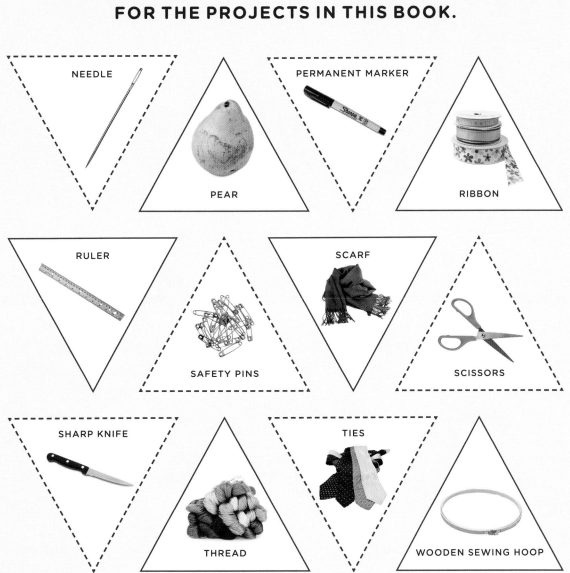

NEEDLE

PEAR

PERMANENT MARKER

RIBBON

RULER

SAFETY PINS

SCARF

SCISSORS

SHARP KNIFE

THREAD

TIES

WOODEN SEWING HOOP

PEAR
STAMP SCARF

Create a Fresh Look with Fruit!

1 Cut the pear in half.

2 Lay the scarf on the cardboard.

3 Brush fabric paint on the flat side of a pear half.

4 Stamp the painted pear on the scarf in rows. Add paint after each stamp. Let it dry.

5 Add stems with a permanent marker.

Even Cooler!

Use several colors of fabric paint to add more color!

3

4

5

11

PERFECT
HAIR BOW

Beautify Your Hair with a Bow!

WHAT YOU NEED

TIE

SCISSORS

RULER

HOT GLUE GUN & GLUE STICKS

HAIR CLIP

1 Cut the label off of the tie. Open the tie by cutting any threads in the center. Remove any extra fabric inside the tie. Cut a rectangle out of the tie fabric. Make it $10\frac{1}{2}$ by $4\frac{1}{2}$ inches (27 by 12 cm). Cut out a second rectangle. Make it $1\frac{1}{4}$ by $2\frac{1}{2}$ inches (3 by 6 cm).

2 Lay the large rectangle face down. Fold the long sides in so they meet in the middle.

3 Fold the ends in so they meet in the middle. Glue the folds in place.

4 Lay the small rectangle face down. Fold the long sides in so they meet in the middle.

5 Pinch the middle of the larger rectangle. Wrap the smaller rectangle around the middle of the larger rectangle. Glue the ends of the small rectangle in place. Glue a hair clip to the back of the bow. Let the glue dry.

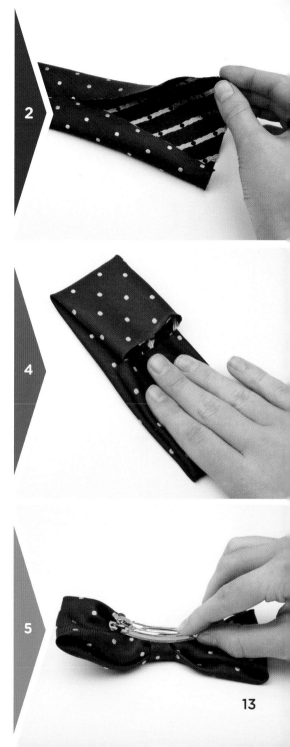

13

BEADED
NECKLACE

Tie a Necklace up in Knots!

14

1. Cut the label off of the tie. Open the tie by cutting any threads in the center. Remove any extra fabric inside the tie. Trim the width of the tie to 3 inches (8 cm). Cut off the ends to form a long rectangle.

2. Lay the rectangle face up. Fold it in half lengthwise. Sew the sides together to make a tube. Turn the tube right side out.

3. Put a bead inside the tube. Push it to the center. Tie the fabric in a knot on each side of the bead.

4. Put a bead in each end of tube. Push them against the knots. Tie a knot on the outside of each bead. Add the last two beads the same way.

5. Fold the fabric into the tube at one end. Cut a piece of ribbon 8 inches (20 cm) long. Glue one end of the ribbon inside the tube. Put hot glue on the outside of the tube. Fold the corners of the tube onto the glue.

6. Repeat step 5 with the other end of the tube. Let the glue dry.

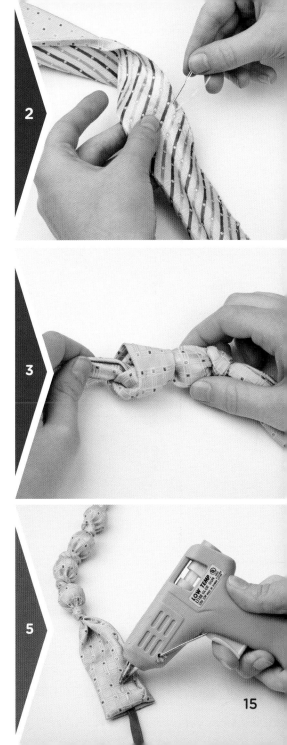

WRISTLET
WALLET

Make a Cute Cash Carrier!

WHAT YOU NEED

TIE
MEASURING TAPE
SCISSORS
NEEDLE
THREAD
SAFETY PIN
HOOK & LOOP DOT

16

1 Cut the tie 11 inches (28 cm) from the wide end. Cut off the label. Cut the tie 10 inches (25 cm) from the narrow end. **Discard** the middle of the tie.

2 Thread the needle. Tie a knot in one end of the thread. Fold the cut end of the wide part of the tie up $1/4$ inch (.5 cm). Push the needle up through all layers of fabric. Pull until the knot hits the fabric. Bring the needle around the edge. Push the needle up through the fabric again. Knot the thread. Trim off the extra thread. Sew the other side of the fold the same way

3 Fold the sewn end up to the bottom of the tie's point. Sew the left side together.

4 Fold the narrow part of the tie in half crosswise. Place the ends between the folds on the right side. Pin them in place.

5 Sew the right side together. Make sure to sew through the tie ends. Remove the pin.

6 Add a hook and loop dot to hold the flap closed.

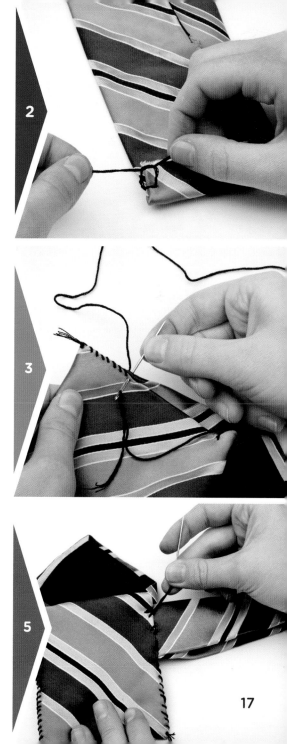

17

FANtastic
VEST

Find a New Vest in Your Old Clothes!

WHAT YOU NEED

BELT

SCISSORS

RULER

IRON-ON FUSING WEB

JERSEY SCARF

IRON

1 Cut off the buckle end of the belt.

2 Place fusing web along the middle 6 inches (15 cm) of the belt.

3 Lay the edge of the scarf over the fusing web. Make sure the scarf is centered. Iron it in place following the instructions on the package.

4 Lay one end of the scarf along the belt. Leave 3 inches (8 cm) between it and the middle section of the scarf. It's okay if the end of scarf sticks out past the belt.

5 Use fusing web to attach the end of the scarf to the belt.

6 Repeat steps 4 and 5 with the other end of the scarf and belt.

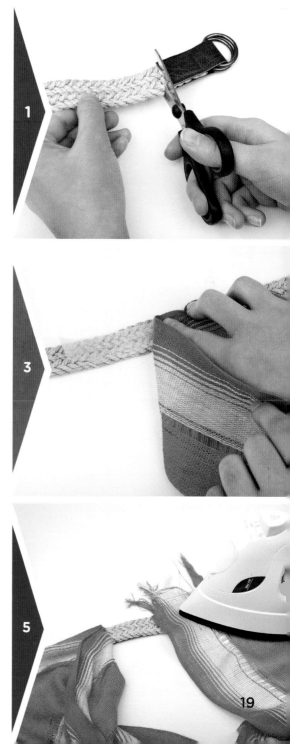

19

EASY
BELTED Tie

Make a Simple Belt Fast!

1 Measure around your waist where you wear your jeans. Add 10 inches (25 cm) to the measurement.

2 Lay the tie out flat. Measure the total length from step 1 starting at the wide end of the tie. Cut the tie at the end of the measurement. **Discard** the narrow end of the tie.

3 Lay the tie face down. Fold the cut end up $1/4$ inch (.5 cm). Glue the fold in place. Let it dry.

4 Put the glued end of the tie through both D rings. Fold the end over the D rings. Glue the fold in place. Let it dry.

5 Wrap the belt around your waist. Stick the wide end of the tie through both D rings. Then stick it back through the second D ring.

21

FOLDED
SCARF BAG

Pursue Your Dreams with a Fun Purse!

TOOLS

6-INCH (15 CM) WOODEN SEWING HOOP

HOT GLUE GUN & GLUE STICKS

RIBBON

SCISSORS

SCARF

SAFETY PINS

MEASURING TAPE

MARKER

IRON-ON FUSING WEB

IRON

1 Separate the hoops. Tighten the knob on the larger hoop as small as it will go.

2 Glue the end of the ribbon to the inside of the smaller hoop.

3 Wrap the ribbon around the hoop. Put a dot of hot glue on the inside of the hoop every few inches.

4 Keep wrapping until the hoop is covered. Cut the ribbon. Glue the end to the inside of the hoop.

CONTINUED ON NEXT PAGE

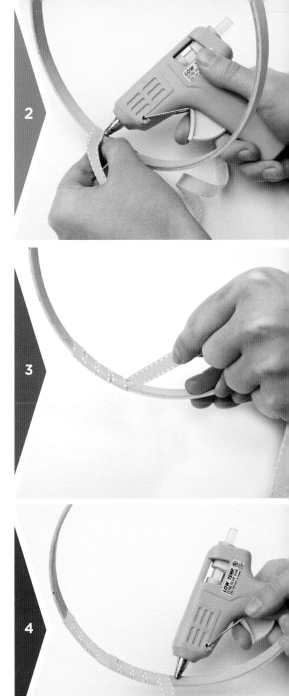

5 Repeat steps 2 through 4 to wrap ribbon around the larger hoop.

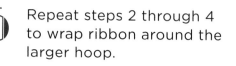

6 Cover the hoop as close to the knob as possible.

7 Fold one side of the scarf around the smaller hoop. Use safety pins to hold it in place. Add a safety pin about every $\frac{1}{2}$ inch (1 cm).

8 Wrap the opposite side of the scarf around the larger hoop the same way. Turn the hoop until the knob is inside the folded edge.

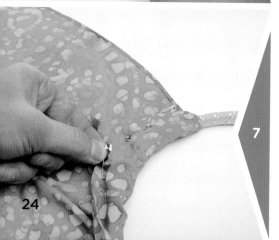

9 Fold the scarf in half. Make a small mark at the fold on each side of the scarf.

10 Make a mark on each side of the scarf 2 inches (5 cm) from the hoops.

11 Put fusing web between the layers along one edge of the scarf. It should be between the two marks. Iron it in place following the instructions on the package.

12 Repeat step 11 on the other side of the scarf.

25

REVERSIBLE
SKIRT

Refashion Your Scarves into Skirts!

TOOLS

RIBBON, 1 INCH
(2.5 CM) WIDE

RULER

SCISSORS

2 LARGE COTTON
SCARVES

IRON-ON FUSING WEB

IRON

NEEDLE

THREAD

1 Cut a piece of ribbon 36 inches (91 cm) long. Then cut the ribbon in half.

2 Lay one scarf out **horizontally**. Cut a 1-inch (2.5 cm) piece of fusing web. Place it near the upper right corner of the scarf. Lay the end of a ribbon over the fusing web. Iron it in place following the instructions on the package.

3 Iron the other ribbon to the upper left corner of the scarf the same way.

4 Lay fusing web along the long edge of the scarf.

CONTINUED ON NEXT PAGE

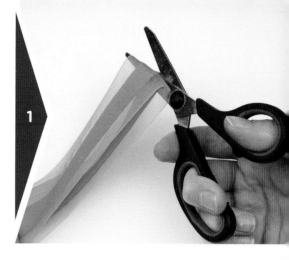

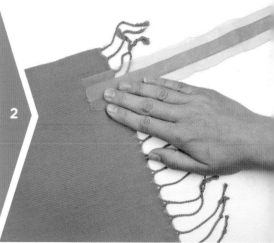

27

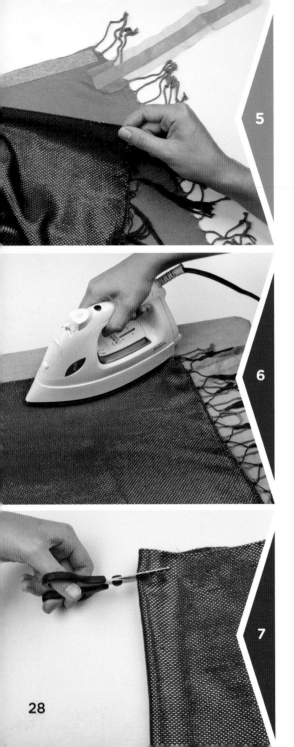

5 Lay the second scarf on top of the first scarf. Line up the edges over the fusing web.

6 Iron it in place following the instructions on the package.

7 Fold the scarves in half so the ribbons lie on top of each other. Measure $1\frac{1}{4}$ inches (3 cm) down from the fused edge. Make a 2-inch (5 cm) cut in the fold through all of the layers.

28

8 Thread the needle. Tie a knot in one end of the thread.

9 Unfold the scarves. Sew around the edge of the cut. Knot the thread near the fabric. Cut the thread near the knot.

10 Trim the ends of the ribbons if they are **frayed**.

11 Wrap the skirt around your waist. Slide the right ribbon through the slit. Bring it around to the front. Tie it to the other ribbon.

29

CONCLUSION

Congratulations! You've just completed some fun projects using scarves and ties. But don't stop here! Take what you've learned to the next step. Try out your own ideas for refashioning neckwear. Make something **unique** and totally you!

Check out the other books in this series. Learn how to refashion jeans, **hardware**, T-shirts, and more.

Get crafting today!

GLOSSARY

DESIGN – a decorative pattern or arrangement.

DISCARD – to throw away.

FRAY – to unravel or become worn at the edge.

HARDWARE – metal tools and supplies used to build things.

HORIZONTALLY – in the same direction as the ground, or side-to-side.

PERMISSION – when a person in charge says it's okay to do something.

TRANSFORM – to change something completely.

UNIQUE – different, unusual, or special.

Websites

To learn more about Cool Refashion, visit **booklinks.abdopublishing.com**. These links are routinely monitored and updated to provide the most current information available.

31

INDEX